A one-act musical
Music by Zachary Israel Nobile Kampler
Book & Lyrics by Rocco Natale

Inspired by Ernest Thayer's "Casey at the Bat"

www.youthplays.com
info@youthplays.com
424-703-5315

CAST OF CHARACTERS

K.C.

RAMONA

PRISSY VON MISSY

LOLLY

SAMANTHA

ABBIE

JONAH

WILL

DAVID

HENRY

DAD

BASEBALL PLAYERS, TEACHERS, KIDS

PRODUCTION NOTES

You will notice three distinct markings in the script: *italicized*, CAPS and <u>underlining</u>.

This is a system we developed with our performers during the first workshop of the show. Any word in *italics* is meant to be emphasized at the actor's discretion (slowed down, inflected, etc.). Words which appear in ALL CAPS indicate that the word is meant to be spoken loudly, and when <u>underlining</u> appears, it means the word is critical to the thought and should be heightened. <u>Underlined</u> words tend to be where the character's thought process "lands."

In our first production, we found that this system of differentiating critical words helped our actors get laughs on joke-lines and distinguish one character from another.

WITH THANKS TO...

The cast of the Cherry Lane Theatre production: Alison Santiano, Sophia Georgas, Christina Keating, Daisy Gray, Lily Bartels, Sofia Degani, Bella Berrocal, Julia Bibeault, Natalie Anibal, Andrew Restieri & Patty Kohn. Gratitude to Bob DeAngelo, Sukie McFadden & Don Palmer at The Boys & Girls Club of Greenwich.

MUSICAL NUMBERS

Overture
Mudville: Company
Like Us: The Kids
Ten Thousand Lights: K.C.
Horrible, Terrible, Awful: Will & The Kids
Baseball Ballet: The Kids
T-E-A-M: K.C. & The Kids
Ten Thousand Lights (Reprise): K.C. & Prissy
Like Us (Reprise): Prissy
The Blog Song: Ramona
T-E-A-M (Reprise): Samantha, Henry, David & Lolly
Together We Can: Prissy, K.C. & Company

MUSIC: Overture

SCENE 1

(The OVERTURE ends. The lights come up on RAMONA S. BARRY, age 12. She looks at the audience as she writes her blog. Mudville Elementary School. Lunch.)

RAMONA: Dear Readers, this is Ramona S. Barry with an important announcement. Today's lunch is fish sticks with a side of cold mashed potatoes. After petitioning for a week, the third grade class has successfully convinced Mrs. Bennet to move the spelling quiz from Tuesday to Thursday. In related news, the sixth grade classroom hamster, Pinwheel, will be celebrating his fourth birthday. Remember to stop by Mr. Winston's room to wish Pinwheel many happy returns. Other than this breaking news...not much is happening in Mudville.

Mudville

KIDS: WELCOME TO MUDVILLE
SPECIAL, WERE NOT
AUGUST IS FREEZING
DECEMBER IS HOT
THIS IS THE TOWN THAT
THE MAP FORGOT
LOOK AROUND AND YOU'RE THERE
WELCOME TO NOWHERE

(PRISSY VON MISSY, the popular girl, enters with her lunch on a tray. She is followed by LOLLY, SAMANTHA and ABBIE, all of whom want to be just like her.)

PRISSY: Can you believe Ms. Jones gave me a "B" on my macaroni sculpture!?

LOLLY: You were robbed!

SAMANTHA: Who cares about macaroni sculptures anyway?

ABBIE: Do you guys want to go to the mall after school?

PRISSY: We have baseball practice!

LOLLY: Besides, the mall closed three years ago.

KIDS: WELCOME TO MUDVILLE
DIRTY AND SMALL
WE DON'T HAVE A SWEET SHOP
OR EVEN TOWN HALL
IF YOU LIKE BORING
THEN WE HAVE IT ALL
LOUISVILLE CAN'T COMPARE
WELCOME TO NOWHERE

ABBIE: We could drive to Mottville. They have a movie theatre.

SAMANTHA: We can't drive anywhere.

LOLLY: We're in third grade.

PRISSY: Face it. There's nothing to do in this town.

KIDS: WE USED TO BE A LEADER
WE USED TO SETTLE THE SCORE
WE USED TO HAVE A BASEBALL TEAM
WE DON'T ANYMORE

WELCOME TO MUDVILLE
DON'T BE NAIVE
MUDVILLE IS PRETTY
WHEN YOU CAN LEAVE
EVEN SANTA WON'T STOP
ON CHRISTMAS EVE
LOOK AROUND YOU'RE THERE
WELCOME TO NOWHERE

WELCOME TO NOWHERE
WELCOME TO NOWHERE

(Ramona enters as the song ends.)

SAMANTHA: Any news, Ramona?

PRISSY: News in this town? Ha!

LOLLY: Yeah. News in this town?! Ha!

PRISSY: Mudville hasn't made the news since 1953.

LOLLY: Yeah. Mudville hasn't made the news since 1953. Ha!

PRISSY: If you want news —

LOLLY: Yeah! If you want news —

PRISSY: Okay. You HAVE to stop repeating me.

RAMONA: It just so happens I have the scoop of the year.

SAMANTHA: What is it?

RAMONA: You'll just have to read my blog.

SAMANTHA: Can't you tell us?

ABBIE: Just this once.

PRISSY: I don't believe you have any news.

RAMONA: I do so.

PRISSY: Prove it.

RAMONA: A good journalist never reveals a story prematurely.

PRISSY: You're not a journalist. You write a blog.

LOLLY: Yeah. You're not a journalist. You write a blog.

(Prissy stares at her.)

Sorry.

RAMONA: Alright. Just this once. Mudville Elementary has a new member of the student body.

LOLLY: Did Steven Kinley fail math again?

RAMONA: No. A <u>new</u> student. From New York City.

LOLLY, SAMANTHA, ABBIE: Ohhhhhhh New York City.

PRISSY: I don't believe it.

(HENRY, WILL, DAVID & JONAH enter with their lunches.)

HENRY: Don't believe what?

ABBIE: We're getting a new student.

DAVID: Did Steven fail math again?

RAMONA: Uhhhh! No. A girl. From New York.

JONAH: Cool...where is New York?

WILL: *(Asking Ramona:)* How do you know?

RAMONA: She moved next door to me. She lives with her dad.

PRISSY: Uhhhhh a new girl...from New York...in Mudville?! I don't believe it!

RAMONA: See for yourself.

(Ramona pulls out her phone. The kids gather around.)

We're friends on Facepage.

DAVID: Well, I'll be.

WILL: No way!

JONAH: What's her name?

RAMONA: Kelli Connors, but she goes by K.C.

Like Us

I HEARD SHE COMES FROM NEW YORK CITY
I HEARD SHE COMES FROM THERE
I HEARD HER MOM'S IN DELAWARE

PRISSY: DELA-I-DON'T-CARE
SHE LOOKS SO STRANGE
SHE THINKS SHE'S COOL
SHE'LL NEVER FIT IN AT OUR SCHOOL

I DON'T KNOW ENOUGH TO SAY FOR SURE
BUT I KNOW ENOUGH TO KNOW
THAT SHE ISN'T LIKE US
NO, SHE ISN'T LIKE US
SO, DON'T BOTHER TO SAY HELLO

LOLLY: I BET HER HAIR HAS COOTIES
I BET HER TEETH HAVE PLAQUE
I BET HER CLOTHES ARE HAND-ME-DOWNS
I WISH THAT SHE WOULD PACK
I BET HER SOCKS HAVE HOLES IN THEM
HER UNDERWEAR AS WELL
DRINKS WATER FROM THE TOILET
AND HER FEET HAVE GOT TO SMELL

KIDS: I DON'T KNOW ENOUGH TO SAY FOR FACT
BUT I KNOW WHAT I BELIEVE
THAT SHE ISN'T LIKE US
NO, SHE ISN'T LIKE US
SO, I WISH THAT SHE WOULD LEAVE

ABBIE: I BET HER BACK IS HAIRY
I BET HER SHOES ARE OLD
I BET HER CLOTHES ARE HAND-ME-DOWNS
AND COVERED IN GREEN MOLD
I BET HER BOOKS HAVE HOLES IN THEM

HER UNDERWEAR AS WELL
DRINKS WATER FROM THE TOILET
AND I'D GUESS THAT SHE CAN'T SPELL

KIDS: I DON'T KNOW ENOUGH TO SAY FOR FACT
BUT I KNOW ENOUGH TO KNOW
THAT SHE ISN'T LIKE US
NO, SHE ISN'T LIKE US
THAT GIRL REALLY SHOULD GO

(A bell rings. The kids go back to class. K.C. enters with her DAD.)

K.C.: What if they don't like me?

DAD: Not like you? How could anyone not like you?

K.C.: You're just saying that because I'm your daughter.

DAD: Even if you weren't my daughter—you'd still be my favorite person.

(Dad hugs K.C.)

Now have a good day!

(Dad leaves as Ramona enters.)

K.C.: Excuse me. Oh it's you, Ramona.

RAMONA: Hey, K.C.

K.C.: I'm so glad to see you. I don't know where I'm supposed to be!

(K.C. hands Ramona her schedule.)

RAMONA: You have History with me. I'll walk you down.

K.C.: The building is so small.

RAMONA: Small?

K.C.: Compared to my last school. Are the kids here nice?

RAMONA: It depends on what you mean by "nice."

K.C.: Oh no!

RAMONA: They'll love you once they get to know you.

K.C.: How long does that take?

RAMONA: Oh one to two—

K.C.: Days?

RAMONA: Years. Give or take.

K.C.: Oh no!

(An idea hits Ramona.)

RAMONA: But of course, if they knew a little bit about you—I'm sure they would love you. It just so happens I have the perfect solution. Are you familiar with my blog? Ramona's Mudville Daily?

K.C.: No.

RAMONA: Well, it's the best...and only...source for all things Mudville. I could interview you. Then everyone would know about you.

K.C.: Would you?

RAMONA: It would be my pleasure. Now let's see...name?

K.C.: Kelli Connors—but everyone calls me K.C.

RAMONA: Age?

K.C.: Eleven and a half.

RAMONA: Favorite food?

K.C.: Broccoli.

RAMONA: Ohhhhh. That's not going to work with this crowd. How about...ice cream.

K.C.: With sprinkles!

RAMONA: Now you're talking. Favorite color?

K.C.: Green.

RAMONA: Favorite holiday?

K.C.: Thanksgiving.

RAMONA: I like your style. Finally—the big one—what do you want to be when you grow up?

K.C.: Old enough to drive.

RAMONA: I mean—a doctor? Movie star? Scuba instructor?

K.C.: I'm going to be a baseball player! You know Mottville stadium?

RAMONA: Do I know Mottville stadium?! They're our rivals. Sworn enemy. They drove Mudville baseball right under ground when they started winning.

K.C.: Well, my dream is to play Mottville.

RAMONA: *(Writing into her blog:)* I'll just skip the details and say "baseball player."

Ten Thousand Lights

K.C.: THERE ARE TWENTY THOUSANDS SEATS
WITH TWENTY THOUSAND FACES
WAITING FOR THE PITCH
WATCHING ALL FOUR BASES
THERE ARE TWENTY THOUSAND FANS
WHO ARE CHEERING AT THE SIGHT
OF THE GREATEST BASEBALL PLAYER

UNDER TEN THOUSAND LIGHTS

THAT'S ME
TIP MY HAT
I HIT THE BALL
THAT AIN'T ALL
I BREAK THE BAT
THAT IS WHERE
I WANT TO BE
CAUSE WHEN I'M RUNNIN'
THERE'S NO STOPPIN' ME

THERE ARE TWENTY THOUSAND CHEERS
FROM TWENTY THOUSAND FACES
THAT'S MY FAVORITE PITCH
RUNNIN' ROUND THE BASES
THERE ARE TWENTY THOUSAND KIDS
NOW HOME PLATE IS JUST IN SIGHT
AND I AM THE GREATEST PLAYER
UNDER TEN THOUSAND LIGHTS

THAT'S ME
I CAN WISH
THAT FOR FUN
I CAN RUN
BACK TO THE DISH
THEN THE CROWD
CAN'T HELP BUT SEE
THAT WHEN I'M PLAYIN'
THERE'S NO STOPPING ME

THERE ARE TWENTY THOUSAND CHEERS
NO, TWENTY THOUSAND SCREAMING
IT'S A GAME TO THEM
BUT IT'S ALL THAT I'VE BEEN DREAMING

THERE ARE TWENTY THOUSAND STRONG
THE BALL FLIES OUT OF SIGHT
AND I AM THE GREATEST PLAYER
UNDER TEN THOUSAND LIGHTS

RAMONA: You should check out our team.

K.C.: Are they good?

RAMONA: I wouldn't say good.

K.C.: Are they bad?

RAMONA: Being a serious journalist, I cannot say...but...off the record...they are terrible.

(The bell rings.)

The little field, after school. Be there!

(The girls exit. The scene transitions.)

SCENE 2

(The Field. Prissy, Lolly, Samantha, Abbie, Henry, Will, David & Jonah get ready to play. The kids practice. They warm up. They stretch. Abbie is singing musical scales as the others get into their equipment.)

ABBIE: Mi-mi-mi-mi-mi-mi-mi, re re re re re re re, fa, so, la, ti.

PRISSY: What are you doing?

ABBIE: I'm warming up.

PRISSY: This is baseball!

ABBIE: Well, I don't want to sprain my vocal chords, do I?

DAVID: Why can't I play first base?

JONAH: Because you're terrible.

DAVID: So are you.

JONAH: Yeah, but you're more terrible than I am.

DAVID: Will...who's the most terrible?

WILL: You're both bad!

DAVID: Well, who asked you?!

HENRY: *(Suddenly:)* It doesn't matter!

SAMANTHA: What doesn't matter?

HENRY: Who plays what. We're going to lose.

LOLLY: Why do you say that?

HENRY: We always lose. We haven't won a game in years!

PRISSY: If you ask me, Henry, you're just being negative.

HENRY: It's a fact.

PRISSY: It may be true, young man—but it's a very immature outlook.

HENRY: Stop calling me immature.

PRISSY: Then don't be immature.

HENRY: What makes you think you're the boss of me?

PRISSY: I'm older.

HENRY: By two minutes!

PRISSY: Yes, and in two minutes—you'll see I'm right.

JONAH: Alright—are we going to play or are we going to argue?

LOLLY: We usually do both.

JONAH: It was a rhetorical question, Lolly! Now I have decided—

(K.C. and Ramona enter. They all look at them.)

RAMONA: Oh. Don't mind us. We're just observing.

PRISSY: Ummmmmmmmmmmm this is a closed practice.

RAMONA: I'm a journalist, Prissy. I need to cover the story.

ABBIE: What story?

LOLLY: Is it about us?

SAMANTHA: Of course it's about us. And it won't be pretty.

ABBIE: Why not?

SAMANTHA: Because we're awful.

DAVID: We're not <u>that</u> bad.

WILL: We really are.

PRISSY: And who are you—?

(She turns to K.C. Silence.)

K.C.: Oh, I'm—

PRISSY: I know who you are.

K.C.: Then why ask me who I am?

PRISSY: What did you say?

K.C.: I said, why did you ask who I was if you knew...?

HENRY: *(Knowingly:)* Uh oh.

PRISSY: Allow me to introduce myself. My name is Prissy Von Missy.

RAMONA: Here we go!

PRISSY: I'm the class president, class secretary and class—

HENRY: Clown—

PRISSY: —Valedictorian. You can't just waltz into my practice—

K.C.: YOUR practice?

PRISSY: Oh yes. Did I forget to mention? I'm also the team manager.

RAMONA: Surprise, surprise.

K.C.: So, you're the one responsible for them.

PRISSY: I am.

K.C.: Do you win a lot of games?

PRISSY: ...sometimes.

HENRY: Never.

PRISSY: Henry!

HENRY: Not once.

ABBIE: In five years.

LOLLY: That's a LONG time.

PRISSY: My teammates and I disagree about the state of our team.

WILL: Oh, face it, you guys —

Horrible, Terrible, Awful

WE CAN'T CATCH A BALL
OR MAKE A PLAY
AT THE START OF THE INNING
WE CALL IT A DAY
'CAUSE THE PITCHER CAN'T PITCH
SO DITCH US TODAY
WE'RE GOOD AT BEING BAD

KIDS: WE ARE
HORRIBLE, TERRIBLE, AWFUL
THE WORST OF THE BEST
IS STILL BETTER BY FAR
THAN THE BEST OF THE WORST
OF US ARE

WILL: WE CAN'T RUN A MAN
OR LOAD BASES
AT THE END OF THE INNING
THEIR TEAM IS ALL ACES
OUR CATCHER CAN'T CATCH
OR TIE HIS SHOELACES
WE'RE GOOD AT BEING BAD

KIDS: WE ARE
TERRIBLE, HORRIBLE, AWFUL
THE WORST OF THE BEST
IS STILL BETTER BY FAR

THAN THE BEST OF THE WORST
OF US ARE

WILL: OHHHH EVERY TEAM HAS THEIR PROBLEMS
OURS ARE WORSE BY LEAPS AND BOUNDS
WHICH IS WHY THE UMPIRE LAUGHS AT US
WHEN WE TAKE THE MOUND

KIDS: HE KNOWS WE'RE
HORRIBLE, TERRIBLE, AWFUL
THE WORST OF THE BEST
IS STILL BETTER BY FAR
THAN THE BEST OF THE WORST
OF US ARE

AND BELIEVE YOU ME
IT'S QUITE A SIGHT TO SEE
THAN THE BEST
OF THE WORST
OF US ARE

PRISSY: Well, if we are—it's NOT my fault. If you could all just follow my instructions.

LOLLY: Yeah. You guys should follow her instructions.

PRISSY: We might be coordinated.

LOLLY: Yeah. We might be coordinated.

PRISSY: It's not my fault that—

LOLLY: It's not her fault that—

PRISSY: LOLLY!

LOLLY: Sorry.

PRISSY: As I was saying. It's not my fault that you can't follow my instructions!

ABBIE: I think we should quit.

JONAH: Quit?!

WILL: No!

DAVID: What would that make us?

SAMANTHA: Quitters!

DAVID: And quitters never win.

HENRY: They never lose either.

(Everyone begins to argue. K.C. goes up to Ramona and hands her a ball. She grabs a bat and runs offstage saying:)

K.C.: Give it all you got!

(Ramona throws the ball offstage. We hear the sound of a bat cracking. The ball flies through the air. The kids stop arguing and turn their heads to look. They are amazed.)

JONAH: Wow!

WILL: Did you see that?

SAMANTHA: Where did it go?

HENRY: They saw that in Mottville.

LOLLY: How'd she do it?

(K.C. comes back onstage.)

RAMONA: They're speechless. That's not easy to do.

ABBIE: What's your trick?

K.C.: ...Hard work? Practice? Determination?

PRISSY: Ughhhhh what I should be impressed?

HENRY: All for K.C. as our new coach? Say, "Aye."

K.C.: Oh, no...I couldn't...

HENRY: You've got to!

SAMANTHA: Please?

PRISSY: Whoa! This has gone far enough!

HENRY: Sorry, sis. Did you see that?

JONAH: She's amazing!

DAVID: She could turn our team around!

LOLLY: I have to agree, Prissy. She's good!

PRISSY: Fine. Let's take a vote! All in favor of Babe Ruth over here — but just remember — my mom will bake brownies!

(The kids all say, "Aye." Prissy walks up to Ramona.)

PRISSY: You better not put this in the blog!

K.C.: Huddle up. Now if you want to start winning you have to work together. Let me see what you've got.

Baseball Ballet

(During this musical interlude, the team shows K.C. their skills [or lack thereof]. Henry throws a ball — we hear a glass window shatter. Jonah and David run into each other trying to catch a fly. Samantha tries to bat and falls flat on her behind while Lolly gets hit in the head with a ball. All the while, Prissy mimes shouting at the team. At the end, the team winds up in a heap center stage.)

T-E-A-M

K.C.: WELL OF COURSE YOU AREN'T WINNING
YOU SHOW NO TECHNIQUE
LET'S START AT THE BEGINNING
TO BREAK YOUR LOSING STREAK

T STANDS FOR TALENT

YOU HAVEN'T ANY YET
BUT QUITTERS NEVER PROSPER
ON THAT YOU ALL CAN BET

E STANDS FOR EVERY
EVERY-ONE PITCH IN
THE JOB DEPENDS ON ALL OF US
IF WE WANT TO WIN

A STANDS FOR ATHLETE
GOOD SPORT IN EVERY WAY
YOU MIGHT WIN TOMORROW
EVEN IF YOU LOSE TODAY

M STANDS FOR ME
CHECK YOUR EGO AT THE DOOR
THERE'S NO I IN TEAM
AT LEAST THERE ISN'T ANYMORE

KIDS: THAT'S A T-E-A-M
TEAM! TEAM! TEAM!
BE A T-E-A-M
TEAM! TEAM! TEAM!

K.C.: T STANDS FOR TACTIC
ALWAYS HAVE A STRATEGY
THEN BRINGING HOME THE GAME
WILL BE LIKE ONE, TWO, THREE

E STANDS FOR ENVY
DON'T BE JEALOUS OF YOUR FRIEND
YOUR TEAMMATES ARE THE PEOPLE
ON WHOM YOU CAN DEPEND

A STANDS FOR ALL-STAR
GIVE IT EVERYTHING YOU'VE GOT
EFFORTS COUNTS IN EVERYTHING

SO GIVE IT YOUR BEST SHOT

M STANDS FOR MORE
WHEN YOU THINK YOU GAVE YOUR ALL
A LITTLE FURTHER
OFTEN HELPS YOU CATCH A FLY BALL

KIDS: THAT'S A T-E-A-M
TEAM! TEAM! TEAM!
BE A T-E-A-M
TEAM! TEAM! TEAM!

THAT'S A T-E-A-M
TEAM! TEAM! TEAM!
WE'RE A T-E-A-M
TEAM! TEAM! TEAM!

(End of scene. Transition.)

SCENE 3

(Blog-o-sphere/Mudville Elementary School. Ramona looks at the audience as she writes her blog.)

RAMONA: Dear Readers, in yet another stunning example of turnaround, the Mudville Nine, our elementary school's very own little league team, has come back with a stunning four-to-six season, thanks in great part to the leadership of new team captain, K.C. She is most certainly to thank for the latest wins. When asked what she likes most about working with her teammates, K.C. said...

K.C.: "Well, everyone's so nice. They've made me feel welcome in Mudville."

RAMONA: When asked to give her opinion of the team's turnaround, team manager, Prissy Von Missy had this to say—

PRISSY: "No comment."

RAMONA: Be sure to check in daily for the latest scores.

(Mudville Elementary School. Lunch. Will, Abbie and Samantha enter with lunch.)

ABBIE: Does anyone want turkey with ham?

SAMANTHA: No.

WILL: I'll trade you.

ABBIE: What have you got?

WILL: Ham with turkey.

ABBIE: Ummmm delicious.

(They swap lunches. David, Lolly and Jonah enter.)

LOLLY: Does anyone have thirty-five cents to spare?

DAVID: What for?

LOLLY: I want to buy a cookie.

JONAH: Have half of mine. *(Breaking off half.)* That will be seventeen and a half cents.

(She eats the rest of the cookie to spite him. K.C. comes in with her lunch.)

SAMANTHA: K.C., come sit here.

(K.C. sits.)

I've been thinking about my fastball.

K.C.: Sam, you don't have a fastball.

SAMANTHA: Which is what I've been thinking about. I don't want to play second base my whole life. I'm already 8, these are my prime years!

(Ramona enters.)

RAMONA: Attention! Attention! Normally, I would make you wait to read it on my blog.

ABBIE: Read what?

RAMONA: The exciting news!

WILL: What exciting news?

RAMONA: Oh, just the most important scoop of this young journalist's life!

LOLLY: Are you writing another article about cargo pants? How many times do I tell you, they're never coming back in style.

RAMONA: The Little League Championship Games!

ABBIE: What about them?

WILL: Don't keep us guessing...

(Ramona hands K.C. a letter. K.C. reads it and jumps up and down.)

What is it?

DAVID: What does it say?

K.C.: *(Reading the letter:)* "Dear Ms. Connors—"

JONAH: Who's Ms. Connors?

SAMANTHA: That's K.C.'s last name you twit!

K.C.: "It is my distinct pleasure to invite you and the Mudville Nine to The Little League Championship Games—"

(The kids begin to jump with joy.)

DAVID: Go Mudville!

JONAH: Who are we playing?

SAMANTHA: Kewsey?

LOLLY: Topeka?

K.C.: Mottville! Mottville stadium! Twenty thousand lights! Just imagine!

RAMONA: It's amazing what a little determination can do.

(The kids scream as Prissy enters.)

ABBIE: Prissy did you hear—

PRISSY: Of course I heard. I'm the first one to know everything.

SAMANTHA: Who wants to go to the art room? I have to tell Mrs. Beekman! She's going to be so excited!

(The kids run off and leave Ramona, K.C. and Prissy.)

RAMONA: Well, congratulations. Of course, as a serious journalist, I try to keep my distance, but if I may say so—YIPEE!!!

(Ramona runs off.)

K.C.: Well, congratulations.

PRISSY: For what? You did it all.

K.C.: You managed the group.

PRISSY: And YOU coached them.

K.C.: True. But you organized the practices—

PRISSY: They listen to YOU.

K.C.: But—

PRISSY: Listen! I just want to eat my lunch in peace. Don't you have somewhere to be?

(K.C. starts off. She turns back:)

K.C.: I don't know why you hate me.

PRISSY: I don't hate you.

K.C.: You do.

PRISSY: I don't hate you, K.C.

K.C.: Then why are you so mean?

PRISSY: Mean?! ME?! I'm the most popular girl in school. Do you know ANY popular girls who are mean?

K.C.: Then...why?

PRISSY: I wish they...listened to me, the way they listen to you.

K.C.: Oh.

PRISSY: I have good ideas too.

K.C.: I know.

PRISSY: Like—the uniforms were my idea, and I had the idea to practice on Saturdays.

K.C.: You did.

PRISSY: But...they're winners now, because of you.

K.C.: They were always winners, I just helped them be a team.

PRISSY: YOU made them winners.

K.C.: WE made them winners. Maybe one dream is big enough for two people.

Ten Thousand Lights (Reprise)

PRISSY: THERE ARE TWENTY THOUSAND CHEERS
NO, TWENTY THOUSAND SCREAMS
IT'S A GAME TO THEM
BUT IT'S MY ONLY DREAM
THERE ARE TWENTY THOUSAND STRONG
THE BALL FLIES OUT OF SIGHT
AND WE'RE THE GREATEST PLAYERS

K.C.: WE'RE THE GREATEST PLAYERS

K.C. & PRISSY: UNDER TEN THOUSAND LIGHTS

(The girls smile at each other. Blackout.)

SCENE 4

(The Connors house. Dad is on the telephone when K.C. enters.)

DAD: Well, that's GREAT news! Yes, sir. I sure will. I'm sure she'll be thrilled. Thank you again. Yes, sir. Good night.

(Dad hangs up the phone.)

Well, are you ready for good news? Guess who that was?

K.C.: Dad. You know I hate guessing games.

DAD: It was Mr. Salanger.

K.C.: Your boss? But, you're never happy to talk to him.

DAD: K.C. we're moving!

K.C.: Again? We just got here!

DAD: I thought you'd be happy!

K.C.: I was just getting settled here—with baseball. I have friends here. If we never stay in one place—how can I make new friends?

DAD: You won't have to make new friends—we're moving back to New York!

K.C.: Oh.

DAD: Isn't that great?! You love New York.

K.C.: I do.

DAD: Just think about ice skating in Central Park! Running up and down the piers—fresh bagels! I thought you would be excited.

K.C.: Do we have to go?

DAD: Yes.

K.C.: But—

DAD: That's final.

K.C.: When are we leaving?

DAD: Next week.

K.C.: NO!

DAD: What's wrong?

K.C.: Next week! NOT next week! The Little League Championship Games are next week!

DAD: K.C. —

K.C.: But Dad — I'll let them all down.

DAD: Who?

K.C.: My friends!

DAD: This is my job, K.C.

K.C.: But baseball is my life.

DAD: I'm sorry. We're leaving next week.

(K.C. storms off. Blackout)

SCENE 5

(The dugout of the Mottville stadium. The kids all get ready for the game in their usual ways.)

ABBIE: Mi-mi-mi-mi-mi-mi-mi, re re re re re re re, fa, so, la, ti.

PRISSY: Abbie, I told you to stop that!

ABBIE: You're not our coach.

SAMANTHA: Let's face it—we're doomed.

JONAH: Don't talk like that.

LOLLY: We are.

DAVID: It's true.

SAMANTHA: K.C. was our best player.

DAVID: Not just our best player—

ABBIE: Our coach.

PRISSY: I may not be the coach anymore, but I am still the manager, and I demand that everyone stop being so sad.

JONAH: Can you demand that people stop being sad?

SAMANTHA: Who cares? We're going to lose! That makes me sad.

DAVID: Big time.

ABBIE: AND we're gonna lose in front of all our friends.

JONAH: Not just our friends—

LOLLY: —twenty thousand people in the stands!

JONAH: That's a LOT of people.

PRISSY: If we just pull together—

WILL: Well, at least *you're* happy.

PRISSY: Excuse me?

WILL: You never liked K.C.!

PRISSY: That's not true.

WILL: Oh, come on, Prissy. Everyone knows it.

PRISSY: Listen. I miss K.C. too. I admit that at first I found her — irritating, obnoxious and surprisingly threatening, but —

Like Us (Reprise)

I KNOW ENOUGH TO SAY FOR SURE
NOW I KNOW ENOUGH TO KNOW
THAT SHE IS LIKE US
YES, SHE'S JUST LIKE US
I WISH SHE DIDN'T GO

If K.C. were here, she wouldn't want us to give up.

(K.C. enters with her dad.)

K.C.: No, she wouldn't!

(The kids go wild!)

WILL: You're back!

LOLLY: I knew she would come back!

ABBIE: She wouldn't leave us.

DAD: She couldn't leave you!

K.C.: We drove all night. Thanks, Dad.

DAD: Anytime, kiddo. I'll be in the stands rooting for you all! GO MUDVILLE!

(The kids go wild!)

K.C.: *(Turning to Prissy:)* Are you glad I'm back?

PRISSY: I've never been so happy to see anyone in my entire life!

(K.C. & Prissy hug as Ramona enters.)

RAMONA: Well, THAT'S a sight I never expected to see! Are you ready?

PRISSY: Ready as we'll ever be.

K.C.: Alright team, gather around.

RAMONA: Good luck, team! We're all rooting for you!

K.C.: We've worked hard. So have they —

PRISSY: —so play hard—

K.C.: —play tough—

PRISSY: —play fair—

K.C. & PRISSY: —and give it all you've got!

(The kids chant "Mudville" as they exit and the scene transitions.)

SCENE 6

(The field. Ramona looks at the audience as she writes her blog. On the stage, the team mimes the game behind her.)

RAMONA: Dear Readers, this is Ramona S. Barry with an up-to-the-minute play-by-play of today's game. Just the facts.

The Blog Song

THE OUTLOOK WASN'T SUNNY
FOR THE MUDVILLE NINE THAT DAY
THE SCORE STOOD FOUR TO TWO
WITH ONE INNING MORE TO PLAY

BUT WILL LET DRIVE A SINGLE
TO THE WONDERMENT OF ALL
AND BLAKE, THE MUCH DESPISED
TORE THE COVER OFF THE BALL

THERE WAS EASE IN K.C.'S MANNER
AS SHE STEPPED INTO HER PLACE
THERE WAS PRIDE IN K.C.'S BEARING
AND A SMILE ON K.C.'S FACE

KIDS: COME ON MUDVILLE
LET'S GO MUDVILLE
COME ON MUDVILLE
MUDVILLE NINE

RAMONA: WHEN RESPONDING TO THE CHEERS
SHE LIGHTLY TIPPED HER HAT,
NO STRANGER IN THE CROWD COULD DOUBT
IT WAS K.C. AT THE BAT

TWENTY THOUSAND EYES WERE ON HER
AS SHE RUBBED HER HANDS WITH DIRT
FIVE THOUSAND HANDS APPLAUDED

WHEN SHE WIPED THEM ON HIS SHIRT

AND THEN WHILE THE WRITHING PITCHER
GROUND THE BALL INTO HIS HIP
DEFIANCE GLEAMED IN K.C.'S EYE
A SMILE ON K.C.'S LIP

KIDS: COME ON MUDVILLE
LET'S GO MUDVILLE
COME ON MUDVILLE
MUDVILLE NINE

RAMONA: OH, SOMEWHERE IN THIS FAVORED LAND
THE SUN IS SHINING BRIGHT
THE BAND IS PLAYING SOMEWHERE
AND SOMEWHERE HEARTS ARE LIGHT

AND SOMEWHERE KIDS ARE LAUGHING
AND SOMEWHERE CHILDREN SHOUT
BUT THERE IS NO JOY IN MUDVILLE
MIGHTY K.C. HAS STRUCK OUT

> *(Blackout. The lights come up. K.C. is sitting center stage. Down and out. Will walks onstage slowly.)*

WILL: K.C., you alright?

K.C.: We lost.

WILL: Yeah. We did.

K.C.: All because of me.

WILL: That's not true.

K.C.: You're just being nice. I blew it.

WILL: Blew it? If it wasn't for you we would never have made it to the championship.

K.C.: The kids are going to be so angry.

(The other kids enter.)

I understand if you all never speak to me again.

LOLLY: Why would we do that?

K.C.: I'm the one to blame.

HENRY: So, we don't get a trophy. Big deal.

DAVID: Who needs a trophy anyway?

HENRY: If you want a trophy, Prissy can give you one of hers.

PRISSY: Sure. I have one for being smart, one for being pretty, one for being humble—

WILL: The point is—

SAMANTHA: We don't care.

T-E-A-M (Reprise)

T STANDS FOR THANK YOU
YOU'VE SHOWN WHAT WE CAN DO
WINNING ISN'T EVERYTHING
WE KNOW THAT THANKS TO YOU

HENRY: E STANDS FOR EVERY
EVERY-ONE PITCH IN
THE JOB DEPENDS ON ALL OF US
IF WE WANT TO WIN

DAVID: A STANDS FOR ATHLETE
GOOD SPORT IN EVERY WAY
YOU MIGHT WIN TOMORROW
EVEN IF YOU LOSE TODAY

LOLLY: M STANDS FOR BASEBALL—

HENRY: No, it doesn't.

LOLLY: Well, there's an m in baseball.

ABBIE: Nope.

LOLLY: It's SILENT!

PRISSY: The point is—you're one of us.

(Dad and Ramona enter.)

DAD: I'm so proud of you, K.C.

RAMONA: So am I!

ABBIE: We all are.

Together We Can

PRISSY: I CAN'T DO IT ON MY OWN
BUT TOGETHER WE CAN
TOGETHER WE CAN
I CAN'T DO IT ALL ALONE
BUT TOGETHER WE CAN
TOGETHER WE CAN

KIDS: THE WORLD IS FULL OF PEOPLE
WHO NEED A PLACE
NEED A SPACE
A FRIENDLY WORD
A SMILING FACE
THE WORLD IS FULL OF PEOPLE
EACH WITH THEIR OWN DREAM
BUT WE ARE LUCKY
SO DARN LUCKY
CAUSE WE ARE A TEAM

K.C.: OH, I CAN'T DO IT ON MY OWN
BUT TOGETHER WE CAN
TOGETHER WE CAN
AND I KNOW YOU NEED ME TO
CAUSE TOGETHER WE CAN

TOGETHER WE CAN

KIDS: THE WORLD IS FULL OF CHILDREN
WHO NEED A PLACE
NEED A SPACE
A FUNNY JOKE
A SILLY FACE
THE WORLD IS FULL OF CHILDREN
EACH WITH THEIR OWN DREAM
BUT I AM LUCKY
SO DARN LUCKY
THAT I'M ON YOUR TEAM

OH, I CAN'T DO IT ON MY OWN
BUT TOGETHER WE CAN
TOGETHER WE CAN
AND I KNOW YOU NEED ME TOO
CAUSE TOGETHER WE CAN
TOGETHER WE CAN
TOGETHER WE CAN

(End of play.)

The Authors Speak

What inspired you to write this play?
We wanted to write **K.C.@Bat** because we realized there was a lack of musicals that featured strong female protagonists. Rocco had always wanted to write a musical based on this poem, and Zach worked diligently to create a sound for each of the characters. Ultimately what inspired both authors was a love of musical theatre. In musicals, you get to watch a character take a journey, and we were ready to write a musical about the journey of a strong young woman.

Rocco was also inspired to work on this play because it was based on a poem. Many plays, musicals and movies are adaptations of stories, fairy-tales, books, etc., but few are adaptations from poems. We felt that this poem in particular had much to say to young people about the power of teamwork and community.

Was the structure or other elements of the play influenced by any other work?
The plot of the play is borrowed from the original poem "Casey at the Bat" by Ernest Thayer. Many of the elements in this musical are new. For example, Ramona is a character that only appears in our musical—but one can conclude that she is based on the unnamed narrator of the poem. In truth, Ramona is a composite of so many of the wonderful student performers Rocco has worked with—particularly his younger cousins.

In our musical, Ramona is a blogger. Observing how many young people use technology to connect with one another inspired this character. We think it is exciting and hopeful that there are so many young people who are creating artistic content through the use of new media. We wanted to embrace this in our retelling, while staying true to the tone of the original poem.

Have you dealt with the same theme in other works that you have written?

No. This is a first for us. This musical deals with peer pressure, girl power and being true to yourself. To date we have not dealt with these issues in other musicals. While we began to write the work, we realized how passionate we were about this cause. Being true to yourself is an important lesson that people of all ages struggle with.

Another issue or theme that we explore in this work is "losing." At the end of the musical, the Mudville Nine lose their game. What makes these characters winners in the audience's eyes is the way they handle losing their game. We believe that it is important to share a story about characters who are proud of themselves no matter what the outcome is. In every incarnation of this work, audiences have commented to the authors on how moved they were by the finale and what it meant to have a work like this speak to students.

What writers have had the most profound effect on your style?

When it comes to American composers, Stephen Sondheim, Cy Coleman, Leonard Bernstein & Alan Menken have been major influences on the librettist/lyricist and composer. Mr. Sondheim (whose works include *Merrily We Roll Along, A Little Night Music* and *A Funny Thing Happened on the Way to the Forum*) was a particular inspiration to Rocco for his use of imagery and rhyming patterns in the lyrics.

Both Rocco and Zach were influenced (as well as fans of) Cy Coleman and the types of stories he chose to musicalize. Mr. Coleman has composed for many musicals that focus on one character *(Barnum, The Will Rogers Follies, Sweet Charity)*, and in our musical, we follow the journey of K.C. as she learns who she is and the true meaning of teamwork.

And of course—Alan Menken wrote the score to our childhoods. From *The Little Mermaid* to *Beauty & the Beast* and beyond, Mr. Menken's music can move an audience like no one else.

What do you hope to achieve with this work?
It is our hope that students all over the world enjoy performing in a live musical. We hope that many of them will have the chance to be part of the exciting world of *K.C.@Bat*. This is a fun little show with a great big heart. When we started writing this show we never imagined that a kids show would be our favorite work to date!

It is truly our belief that students will be able to reflect on their own lives after watching or participating in this musical. Because the baseball team does not win the game at the end of the musical, the audience is left thinking about what it means to be a "good sport." In our history with different productions, each cast has shared personal memories of a time when they wanted desperately to "win" something, but instead lost. Ultimately, K.C. learns that it doesn't matter whether she wins or loses the game—it is what she learns about herself and her friends that matters.

What were the biggest challenges involved in the writing of this play?
Learning about baseball! And making the kids authentic. We spent a lot of time researching baseball for this production, since neither author played baseball growing up. We even had a "word wall" of all the words used in baseball, so that we could have an authentic sound.

Another challenge with writing this play was giving each and every kid a distinct personality. While it is true that every character on the Mudville Nine team is a "typical kid," we wanted to give every one a unique voice and style. Our first cast helped us immensely in developing the quirks of each character. They often made suggestions about what they thought their characters would or would not say.

What are the most common mistakes that occur in productions of your work?
Less is more. Don't stop the show with every number. Just tell a story and your audience will be with you. Additionally, metronome markings in the music are accurate and most often the best way to perform the given song.

AND don't get too caught up on staging. Quite often the most economical movement is the most inspiring. Don't worry about costumes or sets or lights. This show was written to be very friendly toward different theatre companies. When the kids get bogged down in props and costume-changes and blocking, the show loses its charm. It's a purposely and delightfully simple show. Just have fun with it!

What inspired you to become a playwright?
We both love theatre. Zach in particular loves classical music and opera, while Rocco loves classical theatre and musical theatre. We both grew up seeing theatre and being a part of theatre and wanted to tell stories like the stories we have been told.

Playwrights also have the chance to be collaborative, and both authors value collaboration. In other mediums (literature, television, film) the art form is less collaborative. But in theatre there is ALWAYS a collaboration. For example, the actors often offer advice to the playwright on how a scene should go or a director can make suggestions about where the plot should move. The final (perhaps most important) collaboration is between actors and audience. The audience ultimately has the final word. By applauding or remaining silent they will let you know how they are feeling—as a playwright, this reaction is thrilling.

How did you research the subject?
We spent time with kids. We listened to what kids wanted, what they feared, and their hopes and dreams. We also had to educate ourselves in the subject of baseball. Neither of us played baseball nor knew anything about baseball, but felt that this would be a fun and moving subject.

Rocco also did quite a bit of research into the original poem. Since the source material was such a popular entity when it first debuted over one century ago, there is quite a bit of historical research on the poem and the author. This came in handy, as there were a few references in the original poem that Rocco needed help deciphering so that he could write the lyrics to the "Blog Song," which is based directly on the Thayer poem.

Shakespeare gave advice to the players in *Hamlet*; if you could give advice to your cast what would it be?
Have a LOT of fun. LOTS of it. Cause if you're having fun—so will your audience!

And…trust the journey of the play. Each time we have seen this work in front of an audience, it has not failed to move our theatregoers. At its heart, *K.C.@Bat* is a very simple story about dedication, friendship and believing in yourself. Each character has their own journey. Prissy, for example, learns to share the spotlight. K.C. learns that winning isn't everything, and Abbie learns to speak up for herself. Our advice to a cast would be to focus on what *their* character learns throughout the play. It's often surprising how much emotion is packed into this tiny musical.

How was the first production different from the vision that you created in your mind?
The first production far exceeded any vision we could have had for the play. It was funny, smart and quick. Audiences loved it and the amazingly talented kids we worked with came into rehearsal humming the music. We were so fortunate that kids really understood Mudville and what the show was saying. Ultimately, we learned how much heart this show had.

Technically, the first production had less sets, costumes and props than we had originally imagined. This was great! It taught us what was truly important about the show: the story. The musical worked without ALL the flashy trappings we had imagined.

What we learned in the first production was how much the kids playing each role enjoyed the musical. We never imagined that they would have the kind of dedication for or affinity toward the music and book. They took initiative and worked harder than we could have imagined. The actress who played Ramona even surprised the cast one day by showing them the blog that she had created about the Mudville Nine— just like her character in the play!

About the Authors

Zachary Israel Nobile Kampler (Music) is an active composer, arranger, conductor, and performer. Mr. Kampler is the founder, Artistic Director, and Conductor of the Eastern Festival Symphony Orchestra. A graduate of the Juilliard Pre-College program, he has performed in Alice Tully Hall and Julliard Hall. Equally at home on stage and in the pit, Mr. Kampler has conducted for Nickel City Opera, Crystal Opera, and TAB Productions, in addition to holding the position of Assistant Conductor with the Stamford Young Artists Philharmonic and Tri-Cities Opera. Previous musical direction engagements include *City of Angels*, *The Sound of Music*, *Urinetown*, *The Pirates of Penzance*, and *West Side Story*. Mr. Kampler holds a BA in music from New York University and an MM in Orchestral Conducting, with a concentration in Opera, from SUNY Binghamton.

Rocco Natale (Book and Lyrics) is Newington-Cropsey Fellowship recipient for dramatic writing and research. His adaptation of *Great Expectations* is published by YouthPLAYS. His play *Smoke Signals* holds the distinction of receiving the Siff Grant for educational performance and was developed to tour with Hospital Audiences, Inc. Mr. Natale's work *Room At the End of The Hall* has been a semi-finalist in the Eugene O'Neill National Playwrights Conference and Premiere Stages, and he has had the pleasure of working with Signature Theatre Company, Hospital Audiences, Mirror Repertory Company, The University of Connecticut and Shakespeare on the Sound. Mr. Natale is currently a member of the BMI Musical Theatre Workshop. MA, New York University; BA, New York University, CAS: The University of Bridgeport.

About YouthPLAYS

YouthPLAYS (www.youthplays.com) is a publisher of award-winning professional dramatists and talented new discoveries, each with an original theatrical voice, and all dedicated to expanding the vocabulary of theatre for young actors and audiences. On our website you'll find one-act and full-length plays and musicals for teen and pre-teen (and even college) actors, as well as duets and monologues for competition. Many of our authors' works have been widely produced at high schools and middle schools, youth theatres and other TYA companies, both amateur and professional, as well as at elementary schools, camps, churches and other institutions serving young audiences and/or actors worldwide. Most are intended for performance by young people, while some are intended for adult actors performing for young audiences.

YouthPLAYS was co-founded by professional playwrights Jonathan Dorf and Ed Shockley. It began merely as an additional outlet to market their own works, which included a substantial body of award-winning published and unpublished plays and musicals. Those interested in their published plays were directed to the respective publishers' websites, and unpublished plays were made available in electronic form. But when they saw the desperate need for material for young actors and audiences—coupled with their experience that numerous quality plays for young people weren't finding a home—they made the decision to represent the work of other playwrights as well. Dozens and dozens of authors are now members of the YouthPLAYS family, with scripts available both electronically and in traditional acting editions. We continue to grow as we look for exciting and challenging plays and musicals for young actors and audiences.

About ProduceaPlay.com

Let's put up a play! Great idea! But producing a play takes time, energy and knowledge. While finding the necessary time and energy is up to you, ProduceaPlay.com is a website designed to assist you with that third element: knowledge.

Created by YouthPLAYS' co-founders, Jonathan Dorf and Ed Shockley, ProduceaPlay.com serves as a resource for producers at all levels as it addresses the many facets of production. As Dorf and Shockley speak from their years of experience (as playwrights, producers, directors and more), they are joined by a group of award-winning theatre professionals and experienced teachers from the world of academic theatre, all making their expertise available for free in the hope of helping this and future generations of producers, whether it's at the school or university level, or in community or professional theatres.

The site is organized into a series of major topics, each of which has its own page that delves into the subject in detail, offering suggestions and links for further information. For example, Publicity covers everything from Publicizing Auditions to How to Use Social Media to Posters to whether it's worth hiring a publicist. Casting details Where to Find the Actors, How to Evaluate a Resume, Callbacks and even Dealing with Problem Actors. You'll find guidance on your Production Timeline, The Theater Space, Picking a Play, Budget, Contracts, Rehearsing the Play, The Program, House Management, Backstage, and many other important subjects.

The site is constantly under construction, so visit often for the latest insights on play producing, and let it help make your play production dreams a reality.

More from YouthPLAYS

Great Expectations by Rocco Natale
Drama. 75-90 minutes. 1-5 males, 1-7 females (4-8 performers possible).

In this new adaptation of Charles Dickens' classic novel, a young orphan boy named Pip is made rich by a mysterious benefactor who believes in Pip's "great expectations." Pip imagines the eccentric Miss Havisham has made his fortune, but all is not as it appears. Can Pip solve the mystery of his own circumstances and win the affections of the beautiful Estella? Love triumphs in this story of the human heart.

Outside the Box by Bradley Hayward
Dramedy. 25-35 minutes. 12 either.

Thinking outside the box isn't always easy, especially when the world requires you to live on the inside. Exhausted from cramming into corners where they do not fit, six teenagers turn things inside out by inviting others to see things from a whole new perspective—outside to a world where balloons change color, brooms become dance partners, and kites fly without a string.

The Old New Kid by Adam J. Goldberg
Comedy. 30-40 minutes. 2-9+ males, 3-10+ females (8-30+ performers possible).

It's the half-day of school before Thanksgiving break, and current "new kid" Alan Socrates Bama just wants to get through the day. But when a new-new kid arrives, things change. Alan has three hours to find the meaning of Thanksgiving, survive elementary school politics, battle for his identity, and spell the word "cornucopia" in this *Peanuts*-flavored comedy for kids of all ages.

Prince Ugly by Matt Buchanan
Musical. About 105 minutes. 4+ males, 3+ female (20-50 performers possible).

Prince William Xavier Hopkirk the Third is under an evil curse. He is the ugliest child in the entire Kingdom—so ugly that children run from his face. There is only one way he can break the spell: he must make one true friend. But how do you make a *real* friend when most children run from you and the rest only stay because the King has offered a reward? Can Prince Ugly, as even his parents call him sometimes, learn the true meaning of friendship?

Murder (Comedy) in Space! by Ed Shockley
Comedy. About 50 minutes. Flexible ensemble of 9-30.

In a zany homage to Inspector Clouseau, with a plot created by middle school students, a bumbling detective and his laser happy cohorts teleport across the galaxy to investigate the death of a futuristic champion of non-violence. The trail leads to the badlands of Mars, where the characters—and the audience—must decide if they will reveal the truth and destroy a fragile intergalactic peace or collaborate in a well-intentioned deception...

The Absurdist Super Hero Fairytale by Deanna Alisa Ableser
Comedy. 30-45 minutes. 5-7 males, 4-6 females, 1 either (10-12 performers possible).

Basiltown is in jeopardy, and its distracted and overly social Hero is off having iced Americanos with his fire-breathing pet dinosaur Fido. With a socially inept Villain on the loose, an Understudy Narrator in charge, and a ditzy but dreamy Damsel in distress, can Basiltown's citizens pull together to save their beloved town while still pursuing their individualized hopes and dreams?

Dear Chuck by Jonathan Dorf
Dramedy. 60-70 minutes. 8-50+ performers (gender flexible).

Teenagers are caught in the middle—they're not quite adults, but they're definitely no longer children. Through scenes and monologues, we meet an eclectic group of teens trying to communicate with that wannabe special someone, coping with the loss of a classmate, battling controlling parents, swimming for that island of calm in the stormy sea of technology—and many others. What they all have in common is the search for their "Chuck," that elusive moment of knowing who you are. Also available in a 30-40 minute version.

Robin Hood and the Heroes of Sherwood Forest by Randy Wyatt
Adventure. 60-70 minutes. 9-30 males, 6-24 females (18-40+ performers possible).

This fresh adaptation of the classic English tale emphasizes a community of heroes as Robin Hood and his friends band together to save the people of Nottingham from unjust taxation and poverty at the hands of Prince John and his longsuffering yet cruel Sheriff. Two gypsy orphans, Maid Marion's handmaiden and a mysterious stranger share a secret that could win the day—or see Robin hanged by morning!

A Midsummer Night's Nap by David J. LeMaster
Comedy. 30-37 minutes. 4-13 males, 4-13 females (7-17 performers possible).

The Bard's classic tale of fairies, lovers and rude mechanicals in only 35 minutes? Three comic narrators help to speed things along, yet still cover most of the action from the original, including the famed Pyramus and Thisbe play within a play, which survives with jokes intact.

Made in the USA
Middletown, DE
07 March 2023

26323768R00031

K.C.@Bat
by Zachary Israel Nobile Kampler and Rocco Natale

Musical. 45-60 minutes. 4-7+ females, 1-5+ males (11-50+ performers possible).

Ernest Thayer's beloved 1888 poem about fictional baseball legend Casey and the town of Mudville springs vividly to life in the present day. When young K.C. moves to Mudville with her father from New York City, she struggles to fit in at her new school. But it's through her love of baseball that she finally connects: an avid ballplayer, K.C. whips the down-and-out local team into shape, leading them all the way to the championship game, where she learns that there are things even more important than winning...

Youth PLAYS

youthplays.com

ISBN 9781620882399

90000 >

9 781620 882399